The **Story** of
Sanitation

GARBAGE GOES OUT!

WHAT HAPPENS AFTER THAT?

by Riley Flynn

CAPSTONE PRESS
a capstone imprint

Fact Finder Books are published by Capstone Press,
1710 Roe Crest Drive, North Mankato, Minnesota 56003
www.mycapstone.com

Library of Congress Cataloging-in-Publication Data
Library of Congress Cataloging-in-Publication data is available on the Library of Congress website.

ISBN 978-1-5435-3111-4 (hardback)
ISBN 978-1-5435-3115-2 (paperback)
ISBN 978-1-5435-3119-0 (eBook PDF)

Editorial Credits
Anna Butzer, editor; Bobbie Nuytten, designer;
Morgan Walters, media researcher; Kris Wilfahrt, production specialist

Photo Credits
Alamy: Chronicle, 10, left 28, EPA, bottom 17; Bridgeman Images: Monte Testaccio, Roma,
11; Getty Images: London Stereoscopic Company, 14, right 28, Roger Ressmeyer/Corbis/
VCG, 15; Newscom: The Print Collector Heritage Images, 12; Shutterstock: AF studio, (arrows)
design element throughout, Andriy Blokhin, 4, Arnain, 9, BigMouse, top 16, BorneoJC James,
24, degetzica, 18, Designua, 21, Flying object, 5, franz12, 19, I WALL, (paper) design element
throughout, Jutinan Jujinda, 25, kaband, 7, Narongrit Suebnunta, (bin) Cover, Nerthuz, (truck)
Cover, petovarga, bottom left 16, bottom right 16, Rawpixel.com, 22, 23, 27, right 29, ,
Shcherbakov Ilya, 1, Thom Hanssen Images, 8, vchal, 20; Wikimedia: Environmental Protection
Agency, top 17, left 29

Printed and bound in the United States.
PA021

TABLE OF CONTENTS

CHAPTER 1
Down In the Dumps....................4

CHAPTER 2
Trash Timeline......................10

CHAPTER 3
Trash Today 18

CHAPTER 4
Trash and the Environment........24

TIMELINE 28
GLOSSARY.......................30
READ MORE......................31
INTERNET SITES 31
CRITICAL THINKING QUESTIONS ...32
INDEX..........................32

DOWN IN THE DUMPS

Moldy leftovers, empty pizza boxes, and plastic water bottles. Food wrappers, Styrofoam, and aluminum cans. In our world today, waste is unavoidable.

Most people toss their garbage in the trash without thinking twice. Once a week we put our trash bins on the curb for the garbage truck. **Sanitation** workers come collect it and take it away. Even though that is all we might see, it isn't the whole story.

If sanitation workers didn't collect the garbage we put in trash bins, it would pile up and make our cities and towns very messy and dirty.

What do you think happens to your garbage after it's put on that truck? Where does it go? Does it get turned into anything else? And what do you think would happen if we didn't have a system for removing our garbage? Would the trash just pile up around us? Would it eventually break down and go away?

About 12 percent of the trash that Americans generate consists of food scraps.

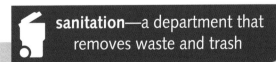

sanitation—a department that removes waste and trash

5

Daily Waste

Only 5 percent of the world's population lives in the United States, but Americans generate 30 percent of the world's garbage. That's a lot of trash! We are sending more and more garbage to **landfills** every year. That's because waste doesn't just disappear. Everything ends up somewhere, and we are all responsible.

READ THE THE FINE PRINT

Do you or your parents read the newspaper in the morning? What happens to it once you're done reading it? Researchers estimate that more than 56 million newspapers are sold daily in the United States. On Sundays over 60 million are sold. To produce the Sunday paper each week, 500,000 trees must be cut down. Recycling one ton of paper saves up to 17 trees. Think about that before you toss yesterday's news in the trash!

landfill—a system of trash and garbage disposal in which the waste is buried between layers of the earth

Sanitation workers drive their trucks to the dump and unload the garbage they've collected.

Garbage Rules

Waste management is the collection, transportation, and disposal of garbage, sewage, and other waste products. The main purpose of waste management is to protect people and the environment. Many materials are normally safe but become harmful if they are not properly thrown away.

Electronics, paint, batteries, and lightbulbs are just a few items that are classified as Household **Hazardous Waste** (HHW). These, and other HHW items, should never be tossed into the trash.

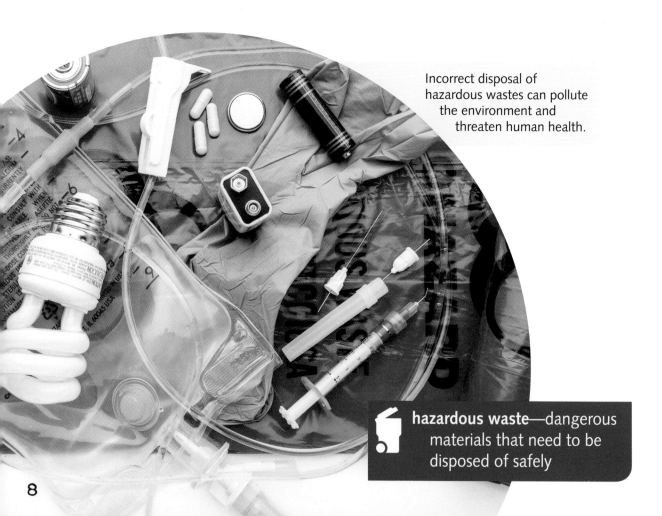

Incorrect disposal of hazardous wastes can pollute the environment and threaten human health.

hazardous waste—dangerous materials that need to be disposed of safely

It is everyone's responsibility to be familiar with their own city's rules for trash disposal. Many cities have limits on how much trash people can throw away each week. Some cities allow residents to pay for the removal of extra trash. This helps pay for the costs of removing the extra garbage.

Some people burn their trash in fire pits. But burning trash is very bad for the environment. It can release poisonous gases into the air. Plus, burning trash is illegal nearly everywhere in the United States.

FACT Burning garbage is harmful to the environment. The smoke produced from burning garbage is much more toxic than the smoke from burning wood. Also, the ash left from burnt waste causes dangerous chemicals to seep into the soil.

CHAPTER 2

TRASH TIMELINE

The first humans did not need to worry about waste management. There was plenty of land and not as many people living on the earth. As the population grew and communities around the world formed, waste became a bigger problem.

The ancient Greeks were the first people to build garbage dumps to keep their cities clean.

Ancient Garbage Dumps

Around 500 BC in Athens, Greece, a law was passed to keep waste outside the city. The law required all waste to be left in piles located at least 1 mile (1.6 kilometers) from the city. These were the first dumps. The Romans developed a similar system about 500 years later. Unfortunately, over time, people went back to throwing their garbage outside or into **waterways**.

Monte Testaccio, a hill made entirely out of clay pots, can be found in Rome, Italy. It is one of the largest landfills of the ancient world.

waterway—a river or any other body of water serving as a way of transportation

Great Britain passed the first law to stop people from dumping their trash out of their windows and into waterways around the year 1300. But this law was ignored by many people, and garbage continued to fill the streets.

Many scientists believe dirty living conditions are largely to blame for the Black Plague (1346–1353). We now know that fleas from rats carried the disease. The rats were attracted to the food scraps and other garbage that people were throwing in the streets. Then the infected fleas jumped off the rats and onto people, making them sick. All across Europe, more than 75 million people died during the Black Plague.

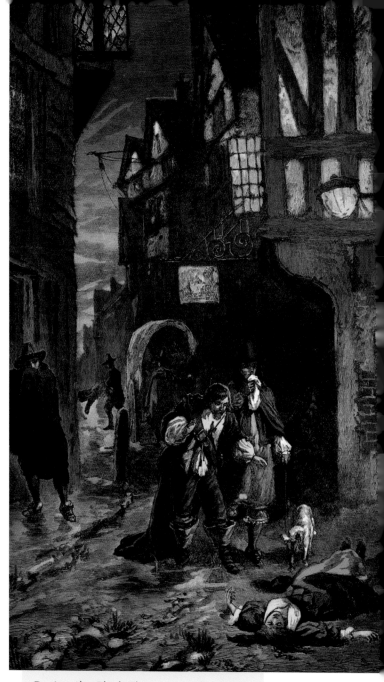

During the Black Plague, people were dying in the streets. Nearly one in three people in Europe died from the disease.

EARLY TRASH COLLECTORS

In 1354 King Edward III ordered that waste on the streets would be cleaned up once a week, so the first garbagemen positions, called Rakers, were created. Rakers collected the garbage from the streets and took it away from the city. However, most of the garbage was still thrown into local rivers.

From the 1300s to the 1700s, deadly diseases continued to **infect** people around the world. By the mid-1700s, people started looking for better ways to get rid of waste. Europeans and American colonists began to dig holes and bury their garbage. However, this did not stop all of the health problems because the buried waste **contaminated groundwater**. This led to unsafe drinking water.

infect—to cause disease by introducing germs or viruses

contaminate—to make dirty or unfit for use

groundwater—water found in underground chambers; it is tapped for drinking water through wells and springs

The Age of Sanitation

In 1842 Edwin Chadwick, a British social reformer, published a report on the sanitary conditions of Great Britain. Chadwick believed there was a link between poor living conditions and the increasing number of diseases. Chadwick recommended cleaning the streets and water supplies in London. This started what became known as "the Age of Sanitation."

The idea that **filth** contributes to human illness gradually made its way to America.

Edwin Chadwick
1800–1890

Fired Up

People using the first dumps discovered something interesting. The garbage in the dumps would sometimes burst into flames. Scientists discovered that the mix of rotting waste created a gas called methane. The methane caused the waste to burst into flames. Methane is dangerous, but people noticed that burning waste turned the garbage to ash. That meant less garbage.

This discovery led to the creation of the first **incinerators** in the 1870s. Incinerators were used to burn garbage in a way that could be controlled. In cities without incinerators, workers often lit dumps on fire to reduce the amount of garbage.

FACT From 1885 to 1908, nearly 200 trash incinerators were built in the United States.

filth—disgusting dirt or waste
incinerator—a furnace for burning garbage and other waste materials

Large cranes are used to move trash in an incinerator center.

Disposing Hazardous Waste Safely

In the 1900s the U.S. government made many laws about how to get rid of waste. People were no longer allowed to dump waste into bodies of water. Cities started waste removal programs to pick up garbage regularly and take it to dumps.

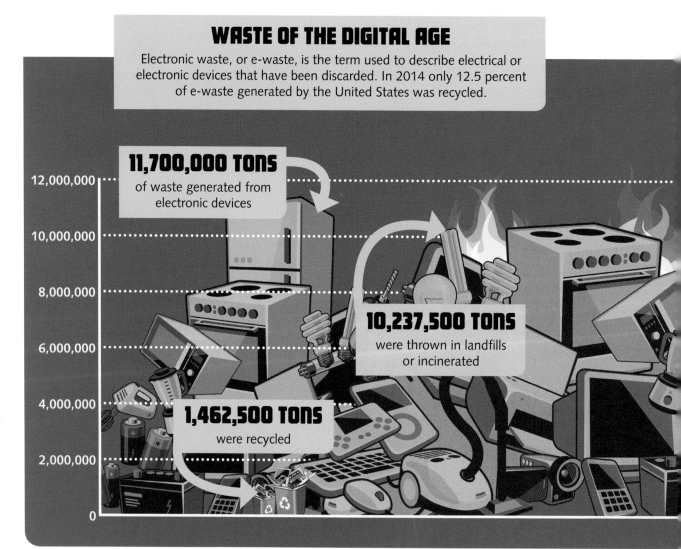

WASTE OF THE DIGITAL AGE

Electronic waste, or e-waste, is the term used to describe electrical or electronic devices that have been discarded. In 2014 only 12.5 percent of e-waste generated by the United States was recycled.

11,700,000 TONS
of waste generated from electronic devices

10,237,500 TONS
were thrown in landfills or incinerated

1,462,500 TONS
were recycled

12,000,000

10,000,000

8,000,000

6,000,000

4,000,000

2,000,000

0

The Environmental Protection Agency (EPA) was founded in the United States in 1970. It was created to protect human health and the environment. That same year the Clean Air Act (CAA) was enacted. This law was designed to control air pollution. The CAA forced most incinerators to shut down. In 1976 the Resource Conservation and Recovery Act was created. This law gave the EPA the authority to control hazardous waste and how it is disposed. Before this law went into effect, anyone could legally dump any hazardous waste into landfills. From these beginnings, our modern waste management system developed.

Before 1976 hazardous materials were not always disposed of safely. For example, smoke from burning old car batteries polluted the air in Houston, Texas, in 1972.

CHAPTER 3

TRASH TODAY

Today the waste we produce is handled in a variety of ways. Sanitation workers pick up trash all over cities and load it onto garbage trucks. This is just the beginning of your garbage's journey.

Every year sanitation workers in the United States pick up 254 million tons of garbage.

Transfer Stations

Sanitation workers take the garbage to transfer stations. At transfer stations, waste is removed from garbage trucks, sorted, and reloaded onto large trailers. These trailers are made to carry large amounts of trash to disposal sites, such as landfills or recycling centers. Think of it as your trash carpooling to its final destination!

In some cities sanitation workers drive to a mixed-waste processing center. There, workers sort garbage. They pull out waste that can be recycled and send it to recycling centers. The rest of the garbage is sent to landfills.

Garbage is sorted at a transfer station.

At the Landfill

Not too long ago, landfills were just holes in the ground where trash piled up. Modern landfills are designed to protect the area surrounding them. A layer of plastic, clay, or a combination of the two is at the bottom of every landfill. This keeps harmful waste from seeping into the ground and damaging the environment. Workers cover loose garbage with a plastic liner or a layer of soil every day. This keeps trash from blowing away or affecting nearby wildlife.

FACT No one knows how long it takes plastic containers to break down or if they ever do. This means it is especially important to recycle plastic. Recycled plastic can even be used to make playground equipment!

Even though today's landfills are designed to keep toxins from leaking into the land, they still release harmful gases into the air. Landfill gas is made up of a few different gases, but about 50 percent is methane. Methane is a **greenhouse gas**. It traps 21 times more heat in the atmosphere than carbon dioxide. The greenhouse gases in our atmosphere make the planet warmer than normal. This affects Earth's weather patterns, creates global warming, and causes climate change.

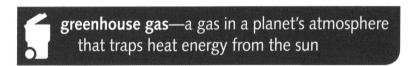

greenhouse gas—a gas in a planet's atmosphere that traps heat energy from the sun

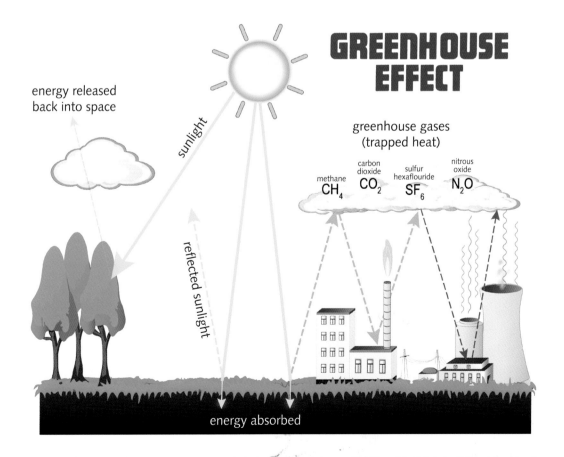

GREENHOUSE EFFECT

energy released back into space

sunlight

reflected sunlight

greenhouse gases (trapped heat)

methane
CH_4

carbon dioxide
CO_2

sulfur hexaflouride
SF_6

nitrous oxide
N_2O

energy absorbed

Recycling and Composting

About 75 percent of garbage is recyclable, but Americans only recycle around 30 percent. It's important to stay informed about the different ways you can help keep Earth clean and reduce waste.

Recycling helps reduce waste. It helps save our natural resources and also save energy. **Composting** is one great way to recycle trash. You can compost more trash than you might imagine. Yard clippings, coffee grounds, paper egg cartons, and even egg shells can all be composted! Fruits, vegetables, pizza crusts, and moldy cheese can be composted too. To try composting, place a mixture of these materials in a bin outside your home. Then let the mixture sit and break down. Your compost is ready when the materials in your bin have turned a dark brown color and smell like dirt.

Today many Americans are recycling and composting, but we need to increase our efforts.

compost—a mixture of rotted leaves, vegetables, manure, and other items that are added to soil to make it richer

The more you are able to compost and recycle, the less trash there is for the sanitation workers in your town to pick up. This means lower trash disposal costs. Plus, composting keeps food waste out of landfills. If there is less waste in the landfills, lower amounts of greenhouse gases will be emitted into the atmosphere.

CHAPTER 4
TRASH AND THE ENVIRONMENT

Landfills keep trash away from where people live, but the areas surrounding these landfills are often in danger. Gases from the landfills can be dangerous for people or animals that breathe them.

Dangers of Dirty Living Conditions

Some studies have shown that as many as 82 percent of landfills have leaks. This means that hazardous waste is leaking into the soil, air, and water surrounding the landfills. These leaks could have terrible effects on the surrounding wildlife and the environment.

Reduce, Reuse, Recycle

Believe it or not, you play an important role in trash management. How much you throw away and where you throw it affects the amount of trash in landfills. The average American throws away 7 pounds (3.2 kilograms) of garbage per day. That is more than anyone else on Earth.

It is easy to remember to recycle things like aluminum and glass, but don't forget about plastic, cardboard, and paper. Each ton of recycled paper can save 17 trees, 380 gallons (1,438 liters) of oil, and 3 cubic yards (2.3 cubic meters) of landfill space.

It's true we have come a long way from throwing garbage into the streets or burying it in the backyard. But we still have a lot of work to do to conserve resources and take better care of our planet.

TIMELINE

500 BC
The first dump is created in Athens, Greece.

1354
King Edward III hired Rakers to remove waste from the streets in London, England.

1870s
The first incinerators are built.

1300
A law is passed in Great Britain to stop people from dumping trash out of their windows or into waterways.

1842
Edwin Chadwick states there is a link between poor living conditions and diseases. The Age of Sanitation begins.

500 BC   **1000**   **1500**

1988

The Plastic Pollution Research and Control Act banned ocean dumping of plastic materials.

1970

The Environmental Protection Agency (EPA) was founded, and the Clean Air Act was enacted.

The first Earth Day was celebrated on April 22.

1996

The United States reaches goal of recycling 25 percent of waste.

1976

The Resource Conservation and Recovery Act is created. The EPA is also allowed to control hazardous waste and how it is disposed.

1900

2000

GLOSSARY

compost (KOM-pohst)—a mixture of rotted leaves, vegetables, manure, and other items that are added to soil to make it richer

contaminate (kuhn-TA-muh-nayt)—to make dirty or unfit for use

disease (di-ZEEZ)—a sickness or illness

filth (FILTH)—disgusting dirt or waste

greenhouse gas (GREEN-houss GASS)—a gas in a planet's atmosphere that traps heat energy from the sun

groundwater (GROUND-wah-tur)—water found in underground chambers; it is tapped for drinking water through wells and springs

hazardous waste (HAZ-ur-duhss WAYST)—dangerous materials that need to be disposed of safely

incinerator (in-SIN-uh-ray-tur)—a furnace for burning garbage and other waste materials

infect (in-FEKT)—to cause disease by introducing germs or viruses

landfill (LAND-fil)—a system of trash and garbage disposal in which the waste is buried between layers of the earth

sanitation (san-uh-TAY-shuhn)—a department that removes waste and trash

waterway (WAW-tur-way)—a river or any other body of water serving as a way of transportation

READ MORE

Flynn, Sarah Wassner. *This Book Stinks!: Gross Garbage, Rotten Rubbish, and the Science of Trash*. National Geographic Kids. Washington, D.C.: National Geographic, 2017.

Richard, Benjamin. *Where Do Garbage Trucks Go?: And Other Questions About Trash and Recycling*. Good Question!. New York: Sterling Children's Books, 2015.

Sawyer, Ava. *Humans and Other Life on Earth*. Humans and Our Planet. North Mankato, Minn.: Capstone Press, 2018.

INTERNET SITES

FactHound offers a safe, fun way to find Internet sites related to this book. All of the sites on FactHound have been researched by our staff.

Here's all you do:

Visit *www.facthound.com*

Type in this code: 9781543531114

 Check out projects, games and lots more at
www.capstonekids.com

CRITICAL THINKING QUESTIONS

1. What is composting? How does it help the environment?

2. Name two Household Hazardous Waste items. How are they harmful if disposed of incorrectly?

3. Take a look at the diagram on page 21. Explain how greenhouse gases affect Earth's weather.

INDEX

Age of Sanitation, 14
air pollution, 9, 17, 21, 25

burning garbage, 9, 14, 15

Chadwick, Edwin, 14
Clean Air Act (CAA), 17
composting, 22, 23

diseases, 12, 13, 14
dumps, 11, 14, 15, 16

Environmental Protection Agency (EPA), 17
e-waste, 16

garbage removal, 4, 5, 8, 9, 13, 16
garbage trucks, 4, 5, 18, 19

global warming, 21
Great Britain, 12, 14
Greece, 11
greenhouse gases, 9, 14, 21, 23, 24
groundwater, 13, 25

hazardous waste, 8, 17, 25

incinerators, 15, 17

King Edward III, 13

landfills, 6, 16, 17, 19, 20, 21, 23, 24, 26
laws, 9, 11, 12, 16, 17

methane, 14, 21
mixed-waste processing center, 19

plagues, 12

recycling, 6, 19, 22, 23, 26
recycling centers, 19
Resource Conservation and Recovery Act, 17

sanitation workers, 4, 13, 15, 18, 19, 20, 23

toxic chemicals, 9

United States, 6, 9, 16, 17

waste management, 8, 10, 17, 19, 26
waterways, 11, 12, 13, 16, 25
wildlife, 20, 25